WHAT'S SO GOOD
ABOUT THE GOOD
NEWS?

WHAT'S SO GOOD ABOUT THE GOOD NEWS?

Eight Essential Elements of the Gospel

Charles Lee Bilberry

authorHOUSE®

AuthorHouse™
1663 Liberty Drive
Bloomington, IN 47403
www.authorhouse.com
Phone: 1-800-839-8640

Published by AuthorHouse   05/24/2012

ISBN: 978-1-4685-6044-2 (sc)
ISBN: 978-1-4685-6043-5 (hc)
ISBN: 978-1-4685-6042-8 (e)

Library of Congress Control Number: 2012904144

Contents

Preface

This book began from a question that I deliberated over during my seminary studies at Fuller Theological Seminary. The question was, "What is the gospel of Jesus Christ?" Initially, you would think this was an easy question. It is like asking a carpenter to sit around and ponder the question, "What is a hammer?"

In a time of depressing headlines where uncertainty is all around us, good news can be very welcome. What better news could there be than, as the old hymn says, "The vilest offender who truly believes, that moment from Jesus a pardon receives"? When Christians refer to the "gospel" they are referring to the "good news" that Jesus Christ died to pay the penalty for our sin so that we might become the children of God through faith in Christ alone.

In order that we do not become confused, there is a difference between the terms gospel and Gospels. The word gospel, as used in the New Testament, means "a good message" or "to announce good news." The "Gospels" are what we call the first four books of the New Testament: Matthew, Mark, Luke, and John. These four books chronicle Jesus's birth, life on earth, death, and resurrection.

Admittedly the materials in this book are a mixture of my own thoughts and those that were borrowed from others. I give credit for the portion found in other published works. This book is not intended to be an official definition of the gospel. It is simply an effort set forth to reveal the understandings that are commonly held by most believers in Christ. Transliterations of certain Greek words are included to simply familiarize the average reader with distinctions.

Acknowledgment

I mentioned to my neighbor Lou that I was writing my second book. He replied, "I didn't know that you wrote your first book. Are you writing it because you have to or because you want to?" It was a fair question because some books are written to advance or preserve the professional academic life of the author. Other books are written as part of an ongoing dialogue in which teaching becomes learning and one's own contribution becomes part of that process. Each time that I teach a class I learn new things not only through the research that I do but through the dialogue I have with students.

I am indebted to many people for many things that made this book possible. I thank God for placing me in His vineyard, where he gave me the vision to share His Word with others in innumerable ways. My wife, Taryn, earns my eternal gratitude for her exemplary work in editing and helping me to prepare the manuscript for publication. She gave some of my awkward phrases clarity and more poetic beauty and showed her usual patience with me during my many hours at the computer. Let me also give thanks to Bishop James M. Rogers Sr., pastor of the Greater New Jerusalem Church, Las Vegas, Nevada, who mentored me as a deacon and minister inside and outside of the church while encouraging and correcting me along the way. He gave me assurance as I transitioned from Greater New Jerusalem Church to another ministry to further pursue speaking, teaching, writing, and missions. After praying with me and giving me his blessings and covering, he said, "You'll do well, but make sure you finish well." To finish well does not mean to reach perfection, but, like the Apostle Paul, it means to keep pressing toward the mark of a higher calling. I must thank Dr. Stan Steward, who gave me the opportunity to instruct aspiring students at Bethany University in Las Vegas. I thank Pastor Sam Roberson of Community Baptist Church, Henderson, Nevada, for continuing to call on me to be an instructor for the Nevada State Congress of Christian Education. The teaching opportunities keep me learning as I help those who have a desire to learn. I want to thank Pastor Jesse B. Bilberry Jr. of Mount Pilgrim Missionary Baptist Church, Baton Rouge, Louisiana, and Deacon Johnny Bilberry (deceased) of Sweet Lilly Primitive Baptist Church, Marion, Louisiana. Despite my humility for preaching the gospel, they help me to understand the true meaning of 1 Timothy 5:18: "You shall not muzzle an ox while it treads out the grain, and, the laborer is worthy of his wages" (NKJV). I want to thank the Canyon Ridge Christian Church family and its leadership for giving me the opportunity to experience the mission of building homes in Mexico for families that are in need. It was an experience that my wife and I will never forget. I thank

Steve Thomas, Mike Bien, and Pastor Kevin Odor for having faith in me to facilitate classes at Canyon Ridge Christian Church and the School of Advanced Leadership Training (SALT) with Hope International University. Finally, I express appreciation to my students in both church and collegiate settings. Their names will not appear here, but many who have contributed to my own learning through questioning, challenging, and believing are themselves now teaching, pastoring, and ministering the good news of Christ. I hope this book will give insight to many who have asked, "What's So Good about the Good News?" And if you should find some of them reading this book, you might ask them, "Are you reading this because you have to or because you want to?"

Introduction

What's the best piece of news you ever received? Maybe it was the day the love of your life said "yes" when you asked, on your knees, if she would marry you. Maybe it was the news that you'd just landed your dream job, the one you'd been aiming at for as long as you could remember. Or maybe the good news took the form of your newborn baby's very first hesitant cries—the sounds that told you he or she was alive and well. Those are all examples of good news. Even if you haven't experienced a lot of good news yourself, you can probably think of other examples, from small pleasant surprises to life-changing developments.

Good news comes in many shapes and sizes. But whatever form it takes, good news is always welcome. We like getting good news. It delights us. Only someone who is extremely cynical—a "glass half empty" kind of person—looks for a cloud in the "good news" silver lining. Most of us aren't that suspicious. We hear good news and rejoice!

Good news often is surprising, unexpected—a twist or turn we didn't anticipate. But when it comes to good news, we all like surprises. Good news can jump out of the shadows and take us unawares anytime it wants to. Have you noticed how often good news occurs in the context of bad news? We are presented with a horrifying bill, a worrisome diagnosis, and the realities of what we actually deserve. Then—"Oops! There's been a mistake. Surprise! It's good news!" Good news gets better when the alternative looks bleak.

I recently went to have a stress test and echocardiogram done by my doctor. The results revealed that there was possibly blockage in my arteries. The doctor stated that there is a 15 percent chance that the test could be wrong, but there is an 85 percent chance that it was right. Further tests were done (CT scans, etc.) by my doctor. Later, I went to his office to find out the results of the latest test. The test showed some plaque buildup but not any blockage in my arteries. The doctor said, "Take these cholesterol pills; watch your diet, and you should feel fine." That was *good news*!

But we live in a bad news world. "I don't love you anymore." "Your position is being eliminated." "You need a new transmission." "You need a new water heater" (which I just experienced). We expect bad news. It hangs over our head like Damocles's sword. According to legend, Damocles was a courtier in the palace of Dionysius II, a king who ruled Syracuse in the fourth century BCE. Like many courtiers, Damocles constantly flattered the king, in the hopes that he would be given a position of greater power in the court. Dionysius grew tired of the constant flattery and asked Damocles if the courtier would like to switch places for a day, to see what it would be like to be a ruler. Damocles eagerly assented, and spent a day being waited on by the king and other attendants. Toward the end of the day, while seated at dinner, Damocles looked up to see a heavy sword suspended directly over his head, hanging by a hair. In a panic, he asked Dionysius about the meaning of the sword, and the ruler explained that he wanted to show Damocles what it was like to be in a position of power, which might seem privileged from a distance to the casual eye but was actually quite dangerous. The sword terrified Damocles into fleeing the court, with no more thoughts of power in his head, and the story about the sword of Damocles became a symbol for the hidden dangers of power. It illustrates the incredible danger that many leaders find themselves in, as they are often beset on all sides both literally and figuratively, making their positions far from enjoyable. The sword of Damocles is a somber reminder that power comes with many dangers attached. Damocles did not really know what Dionysius's life was like until he "walked a mile in his shoes."

We are resigned to the notion that bad news is what we get because bad news is what we deserve. It is tragic that so many people paint Christians as bearers of bad news, messengers of doom, or grim judges of the world's inadequacies. Nevertheless, we must break a great deal of bad news to a broken world. When we warn of the wages of sin and the eternal dangers of unbelief, we are doing no more than telling the truth. And sometimes the truth hurts. But bad news must never be our prime business. If there is anything that should be characteristic of Christians, it is should be our utter absorption with good news.

We serve a Master who majored in good news. He went everywhere preaching it. The crowds flocked to hear him talk about it. Tax collectors and prostitutes (people who were all too familiar with bad news) were drawn to Jesus's joyous announcements of news that seemed too good to be true. Jesus did not change the world with pronouncements of doom and gloom. He changed the world with surprising, unexpected, incredible good news.

This good news changed our lives. We heard a wonderful message that some considered unbelievable and decided to believe it. And we have never been the same since. We have been entrusted with the mission of announcing this good news to a bad news world. It is good news we have been sent to preach, not bad. Jesus wants us to tell it from rooftops and sing it on street corners, exulting in it at every opportunity.

But one piece of news is so amazing and so transforming that it's not just good news: it's *the* good news! It is something so wonderful that every other good thing that's happened to you simply pales in comparison.

So what is it? Here it is:

There is a God; he loves you, and you can know him personally.

That's it! Think for a moment about what that means: it means that there's something more to life than the daily grind. It means that pain, disappointment, and suffering are not the end-all-be-all of your life. It means that somebody loves you without asking anything in return—no matter how messed up your life is and no matter what you've done. This good news is the main point behind the Bible, and it's not complicated. All you need to do to receive this good news is believe it.

All too often believers, by way of their attitude and actions, seem to act as though they have been given a bottle of miserable pills. Somehow they think that they have been commissioned by God to spread their nauseating and negative attitude on everyone else in the world. But if you are a child of God you should have joy in your heart. Sam Shoemaker, a former Episcopal priest in New York, used to say that it is possible to be inoculated with the dead germs of Christianity to the point that you become immune to the real thing. John Bunyan, an English Christian writer and preacher of the sixteenth century, said that when he got saved he was filled with so much joy, love, and mercy that he could hardly contain himself. C. S. Lewis, who is perhaps the greatest apologist of the Christian faith during the nineteenth century, and well known for his works *Chronicles of Narnia*, wrote his autobiography, titled *Surprised by Joy*. He wrote about the joy that ought to be in every believer. Some Christians believe that the more serious we are the deeper is our spirituality. But because you are more serious is no real indication of how spiritual you may be. When there is salvation, there should be evidence of adoration, celebration, and jubilation in your life. We all have distinct personalities, and every man or woman is different. Some people may pat their feet, and some may nod their head. Others may wave a hand or say, "Amen," "Praise the Lord," or "Thank you, Jesus." But if you've been saved, then there ought to be some evidence that you've got a relationship with God.

What is the Gospel?

"Preach the gospel every day; if necessary, use words."

St. Francis of Assisi (1181-1226)

There are passages in the Bible that are like great pieces of art. The longer you look at it the more you see. The more you look at a masterpiece of art the more you will see different shades, tones, hues, subtleties, and significances throughout the picture. So it is with many passages in the word of God. There are passages of scripture that will remind you of the dynamic of a classical piece of music. You tend to become more and more mesmerized the more you listen to it. Each time you listen to the music, you hear a new note or some other melody that you did not hear before. That is the way it is with the Bible. The more you look at it, the more you see. You will discover that the Bible is a treasure of good news. It is a repository of gospel gems.

If you have read any portion of the New Testament you probably are aware that the gospel of Jesus Christ is called the good news. The word gospel is a translation of a Greek word *euangelion*. It is a compound Greek word. The first part of this compound word is *eu,* and it translates to the English word that means good. The second part of this word is *angelos,* which translates in English meaning messenger or to bring. Together these two Greek words mean good messenger. We know it in the English language as the good news. The word gospel is used in the New Testament seventy-seven times. The Apostle Paul is credited with using the word gospel fifty-five of the seventy-seven times it appears in the New Testament.

The gospel is called the "good news" because it addresses the most serious problem that you and I have as human beings, and that problem is simply this: God is holy, and He is just, and I'm not. And at the end of my life, I'm going to stand before a just and holy God, and I'll be judged. I'll be judged either on the basis of my own righteousness—or lack of it—or the righteousness of another. The good news of the gospel is that Jesus lived a life of perfect righteousness, of perfect obedience to God, not for His own well-being but for His people. He has done for me what I couldn't possibly do for myself. But not only has He lived that life of perfect obedience, He offered Himself as a perfect sacrifice to satisfy the justice and the righteousness of God.

The good news of the gospel offers freedom from bondage, freedom from sin, freedom from stress, and freedom from all the pressures of this world. And if you have freedom from these you have the one thing that this world cannot give to you, and that is peace. It is a peace that surpasses all understanding. For those who receive the truth of the gospel, there is an inner peace, which comes from knowing Jesus and applying His teachings in your life. When you are at peace within, then it no longer matters what the world throws at you because it can't affect you unless you allow it to. Peace within in these days of great disaster and troubles is truly great news and a real blessing to all who find and receive it.

But there is so much more to offer in the gospel of Christ. He offers hope for a better life, both now in this world, and into eternity in a place where there will be no sickness, disease, death, or any form of evil.

Too often Christians focus on what we must do rather than what God has already done. Second Timothy 1:9-10 states, "He has saved us and called us to a holy life—not because of anything we have done but because of his own purpose and grace. This grace was given us in Christ Jesus before the beginning of time, but it has now been revealed through the appearing of our Savior, Christ Jesus, who has destroyed death and has brought life and immortality to light through the gospel." There are those who try to expand the gospel out of a sincere desire to help individuals respond effectively to it. "What good is the gospel," they say, "if someone doesn't know what to do when they hear it?" And so they pack into the gospel detailed instructions (sometimes very detailed instructions) about responding to the gospel story in effective ways. Believe. Confess. Repent. Be baptized. Denounce sin, and embrace holiness. Join the right church. Don't drink, dance, or smoke. Learn to tithe, and the list goes on and on.

But there are major difficulties encountered here. The size of the gospel more than doubles. It expands to include not only what God has done for us, but what we must do for God. And the gospel emphasis gets badly skewed. As soon as we allow our response to slip through the gospel door, the emphasis on God shifts and shifts radically. God created us—wonderful! God sent his Son—great! Now, let's focus on what is really important: what we must do, our decisions and actions, and how we do our part to complete the gospel work. The focus swings from God's grace to our behaviors, from his gift to our acceptance of it, and from his purposes to our practices.

Rather than celebrating how God has been at work through history to save and sanctify us, the gospel is reduced to learning and living out the work we must do to be acceptable to him. Discipleship becomes a laborious game of playing "catch up."

When well-intentioned people attempt to shoehorn our obedience into the gospel story, the result is gospel inflation and a misplaced focus on ourselves.

The great difficulty facing the people of God today in regard to the gospel is not the world's stubborn resistance to hearing the gospel but is our inability to articulate it.

It does not mean that we too often lack the courage to speak the gospel or that we miss critical opportunities God affords us to talk about his good news. These are not the primary reasons for our gospel muteness. The heart of the matter is much more embarrassing: we do not speak the gospel because we do not know the gospel, and we do not know the gospel because we have misplaced it among the accumulated subtleties we call "religion."

I often say that religion will get you on Kingdom Boulevard, but it will never get you into the kingdom. Religion allows you to worship your ability to worship. Religion has run off the gospel. The skin has spilt the wine. "Religion" has managed to hide the gospel so effectively that we can no longer see it; we no longer prize it, and we are no longer familiar enough with it to speak a word of good news to a world dying for the lack of it.

This loss of the gospel has radically affected our views of discipleship, the church, and our mission in the world.

1. It has shifted our focus from what God has done for us to what we must do for God.

2. It has forced us to rely on human insight and effort rather than trust in divine grace.

3. It has persuaded us that the Christian life is about incremental improvements rather than radical transformations.

4. It has permitted us to preach much about the church and little about the cross.

5. It has turned us into nervous, insecure, timid churchgoers when we were meant to be a people who turn the world upside down.

Unless there is a recovery of the gospel and a reinstatement of its privileged place in the life of the church, the church will continue to devolve into a weekly assembly attended by polite people who vote and do nice things. Salvation will be reduced to an exchange between ourselves and God in which obedience to heavenly requirements secures mansions in the realms above. And sanctification—that grand calling to share in and enact the life of God—will remain little more than a constant round of motivational speeches leading to renewed efforts at self-improvement.

Dr. Tim Woodroof wrote in one of his many essays on the gospel that the great dilemma of the frequent traveler is deciding what goes into the suitcase and what doesn't. He said, "You can't pack all the comforts of home, or your bags become too heavy—you might be forced to check a bag. But there are some items you can't do without. So I always pack my toothbrush but never my library. Underwear is essential; my seventeen favorite shirts are not. When I make foolish packing decisions, my arms hurt from lugging around all sorts of things I don't really need. When I pack wisely, I travel with nimbleness and grace and always have what I require for the journey."

In packing our gospel bag, we face a similar dilemma. What do we put in, and what do we leave out? Too much, and the gospel becomes unwieldy, bloated, and burdensome. Too little, and the gospel doesn't contain everything we really need for the journey. Packing the gospel is a fine art. It's a delicate balance between including all that is necessary but not one tenet more.

Most Christians are not fine artists. We struggle and stumble in our attempts to get the gospel right. "Does this belong in the gospel?" "Is that really necessary for salvation?" We pack and unpack, arrange and rearrange, and still suspect we've done an inadequate job in the end.

The great temptation (where the gospel is concerned) is to pack too much into it. An expanding gospel has been the characteristic tendency of believers in every age. The Judaizers of the first century wanted to pack Moses and circumcision into the gospel. Believers today insist on including everything from worship styles to views on the end times to charismatic experiences. Into the gospel bag go all our favorite practices and traditions and positions. We fill in the blank ("Unless you _____, you cannot be saved.") with every personal opinion and biblical interpretation that we have adopted over a lifetime of following Jesus.

As a result, the gospel grows long and large and laden. The good news becomes a burden. We drag around all the comforts of faith, every cherished practice, and each denominational distinction—a huge and awkward hodgepodge of beliefs, opinions, practices, and perspectives. Transporting such a gospel wears us out. And transferring such a gospel—trying to communicate it and encouraging others to adopt it—becomes well-nigh impossible. We lose our nimbleness and grace. We lose our confidence in living out the good news. And we lose our evangelistic voice.

Some believers, however, move in the opposite direction, leaving out ideas that are essential to the gospel's character. A shrinking gospel has been a temptation plaguing the church in every generation. The Corinthians of Paul's day loved the bits of the gospel that talked about spiritual power but had little time for the cross—but the shameful, foolish one on which Christ died (1 Cor. 1:18). Many Christians both past and present have preferred the part of the gospel that speaks to loving God over the part that insists we must love each other as well.

The solution has been a little judicious editing where the gospel is concerned. Just a snip here and a slice there. Don't like that part about sin's dominion of humanity? Cut it out! Or the part about the Spirit's active role in transforming our lives? Lop it off! Or the bits about resurrection and final judgment? Take the knife to it! At every turn of the church's history, there have been people all too willing to amputate necessary parts of the gospel story in an attempt to lighten the gospel load.

When that happens, the gospel loses its power. It becomes fuzzy and feeble and formless. Stripped of all shame and foolishness, denuded of anything miraculous or inconvenient, pruned of its bold claims and difficult truths, the gospel ceases to be the good news that saves and the means by which God makes us holy.

In 1 Corinthians 15:1-5, Paul says, "Now, brothers and sisters, I want to remind you of the gospel I preached to you, which you received and on which you have taken your stand. By this gospel you are saved, if you hold firmly to the word I preached to you. Otherwise, you have believed in vain. For what I received I passed on to you as of first importance that Christ died for our sins according to the Scriptures, that he was buried, that he was raised on the third day according to the Scriptures, and that he appeared to Cephas, and then to the Twelve." It is important to note that in this scripture Paul gives his classic clarification and definition of the gospel. He gives us two major emphases and elements to the gospel. The first element is the death of Jesus Christ. The second element is the resurrection of Jesus Christ. The burial of Jesus Christ was the validation of His death, and the eyewitness testimony was the validation of the resurrection. The eyewitnesses saw Jesus postresurrection.

Paul gives us the definition of the gospel in 1 Corinthians 15, and he develops it out even further in the book of Ephesians. He gives us the principles and elements in 1 Corinthians 15, but he gives us its theological significance in Ephesians 1:1-12. When you read Ephesians 1:1-10 you will discover that it is filled with many commas and periods. There are punctuation marks all through the text. But when you read it from the Greek New Testament, you will find that there are no punctuation marks in it. Verses one through twelve are a single, long, and complex verse. John R. W. Stotts said, "When Paul wrote this, he didn't even stop to take a breath or to add punctuations. His words poured out of his mouth as a continuing cascade of adoration." When you look at this pericope as written by Paul you will find that Paul points out eight things that are good about the good news.

2

The Good News of Our Election

"I believe the doctrine of election, because I am quite certain that, if God had not chosen me, I should never have chosen Him; and I am sure He chose me before I was born, or else He never would have chosen me afterwards; and He must have elected me for reasons unknown to me, for I never could find any reason in myself why He should have looked upon me with special love."

Charles H. Spurgeon (1834-92)

E lection is a vital doctrine of the Bible but yet is one of the least understood. The word "election" does not appear in the Old Testament. It is found in only six verses in the New Testament (Rom. 9:11; Rom. 11:5, 7, 28; 1 Thess. 1:4; 2 Pet. 1:10). But the word "elect" (Hebrew *bachir;* Greek *eklektos*) appears four times in the Old Testament (Isa. 42:1; 45:4; 65:9, 22) and sixteen times in the New Testament (Matt. 24:22, 24, 31; Mark 13:20, 22, 27; Luke 18:7; Rom. 8:33; Col. 3:12; 1 Tim. 5:21; 2 Tim. 2:10; Titus 1:1; 1 Pet. 1:2, 2:6; 2 John 1, 13). *Eklektos* is translated to mean "chosen."

Christians have been chosen as God's chosen people. Ephesians 1:4 states, "For he chose us in him before the creation of the world to be holy and blameless in his sight." So what's so good about the good news? First of all, Christians have been elected to be His people. John R. W. Stotts says, "Election is a divine revelation and not a human speculation." He is saying that the doctrine of election was not dreamed up by John Calvin, Martin Luther, or St. Augustine. Election was also not the brainchild of the Apostle Paul, and neither was it the concoction of some overactive religious mind. He is saying that the doctrine of election is a revelation of the mind of God. In other words, God came up with the idea of election. He's saying that before the foundation of the world was laid, God predetermined that we would be His people.

Before the beginning began to be and before there was *chronos* or *chairos,* God chose us as His people. It was a time when God walked out from nowhere, stood out on nothing, caught something, and hung something on nothing and told it to stay there. It was a time when God spoke out and said let there be light, and light came running in at 186,000 miles per second. Before God took the prime rib out of Adam's side and made woman He had predestined us unto salvation. God is sovereign, and He moves and acts according to His own will. The old folks used to say, "He's God all by himself." He doesn't need anyone else because He already knows how to be God.

Prior to man's existence he already held a significant place in both creation and redemption. God knew that man was going to fall before He created us. Yet He created us anyway. He knew that He was going to lift to a level of dignity in redemption that would be greater than the dignity we received in creation.

The Bible clearly teaches the doctrine of election, which is sometimes call predestination. But is also teaches the free will of man. It appears that the two concepts may be a contradiction. If you eliminate election from the Bible then you would erase the sovereignty of God. If you eliminate free will you will obliterate the accountability and responsibility of man. Theologians and Bible scholars have been baffled about these two concepts for over two thousand years. The Bible teaches that both of these are right, but it never tries to reconcile the two. It is what theologians call nonclosure or a biblical oxymoron. The best way to try to understand these two concepts is to understand that the doctrine of election is the divine side of salvation, while the doctrine of free will is the human side of salvation. But it takes both the sovereignty of God and the free will of man to comprise eternal salvation. Throughout scripture there are signs of God's election and how He sovereignly selects one person over another. He selected Abel over Cain. He selected Jacob, the trickster, over Esau. He selected Esau, the younger, over Manasseh, the older. He also selected nations over other nations. He chose Israel over Moab. The Apostle Paul says it best in Romans 9:15-16 (NKJV), "For He says to Moses, "I will have mercy on whomever I will have mercy, and I will have compassion on whomever I will have compassion. So then it is not of him who wills, nor of him who runs, but of God who shows mercy." There is evidence of His electing and selecting also in the Old Testament. Jeremiah 1: 5 (NIV) says, "Before I formed you in the womb I knew you, before you were born I set you apart; I appointed you as a prophet to the nations." This is why we should not compete or be envious of each other's abilities. When you compete with each other you are competing with the sovereign electing and selecting abilities of God. When God gives someone abilities He sovereignly selected to give them those abilities. When you plant a rosebush in a flower garden, it does not try to be a tulip. The job of the rosebush is to be the best looking rosebush in the flower garden. As God's creation, we should try to do the same. Our job is to bloom where we are planted.

The doctrine of election also involves the sanctification of man. We have been sovereignly elected by God to be holy and blameless. Many Christians disagree with teaching the doctrine of election and eternal security because they believe it will produce moral weakness. They believe you cannot tell a Christian that they cannot lose their salvation. Many teach that Christians need to know that they will be put out of the family of God and go to hell if they sin. They teach Christians that they have to live holy in order to keep their salvation. But the Bible does not teach that. You cannot lose what you never had. Salvation is a free gift. A gift is something that was freely given to you. If you didn't have it, then you cannot lose it. Paul says, "That is why I am suffering as I am. Yet this is no cause for shame, because I know whom I have believed, and am convinced that he is able to guard what I have entrusted to him until that day" (2 Tim. 1:12). In this scripture Paul is referring to the day of redemption. Therefore, you cannot lose your salvation because you do not keep it. Another reason a Christian cannot lose his or her salvation is because he or she is in Christ, and the Holy Spirit has sealed a Christian in the Father. In order for a Christian's salvation to be lost, their sins have to get past the Holy Spirit, past Jesus, and then past God in order to get to the Christian.

But yet a Christian is called to be holy. You are to be set apart. There should be characteristics about you that are distinctively different from those that are not saved. The fleshly things of the world should not be dominant in your life. You can have material things, but material things should not become your God because that's not being separated. Sanctification, or living a holy life, should not debilitate us, but it should elevate us morally, psychologically, and spiritually.

Someone may ask, "Why should I bother responding to the call to salvation? God will save me when he's ready." The Bible says that God saves those who place their faith in Jesus Christ. No one is saved without faith in Christ. God has the first move, but the next move is up to you. Henry Ward Beecher, a prominent clergyman of the nineteenth century, used to say that the elect were the "Whosoever wills" and the nonelect were the "Whosoever won'ts." If you are wondering whether God has predestined you to salvation, just answer this question: Have you ever placed your faith in Jesus Christ—and in him alone—for your salvation? If the answer is yes, then I've got good news; you're predestined for heaven. But what if the answer is no? The Bible says that God is not willing that any should perish but wants all people to come to repentance (2 Pet. 3:9). Think about that. God wants you in heaven. He even paid the price of admission—the blood of his Son, Jesus Christ.

I must confess that I struggled with the doctrine of election for many years. Eventually I came to an understanding that has freed me from that struggle. It basically consists of two points. The first point I came to an understanding on was our complete freedom. When you wake up in the morning, you have a choice to get out of bed or to stay in bed. You can put on black shoes or brown ones. When you get in your car, you are free to drive to work, or you can drive to Los Angeles if you'd like. Every decision you make is a free choice. By that I simply mean that you do not feel constrained by some divine power that forces you to eat at Burger King instead of McDonald's.

The second point that I came to understand is that God sees and knows everything you do. He hears everything you say. He will someday judge you for all of it. Nothing escapes him. Everything is transparent before his eyes. Yes, you have free will, but you are 100 percent responsible for every choice you make—that includes the choices you make in the words you say and the thoughts you think. He won't just judge the "big" things; he's going to judge the "little" ones too.

So what is the good news about election? Salvation is of the Lord. It is a work of God from beginning to end. Our choice is a free choice, but it is made possible only by God's Spirit enabling us to believe and be saved. Someone has illustrated the truth this way. Think of the gate of heaven, and above it is a large sign, "Whosoever will let him come." As you pass through the gate, you look back, and from the inside the sign reads, "Chosen before the foundation of the world." Or to say it another way: "He doesn't make you go against your will; he just makes you willing to go."

3

The Good News of Our Adoption

"Nobody is born into this world a child of the family of God. We are born as children of wrath. The only way we enter into the family of God is by adoption, and that adoption occurs when we are united to God's only begotten Son by faith. When by faith we are united with Christ, we are then adopted into that family of whom Christ is the firstborn."

R. C. Sproul (1939—)

T he Apostle Paul says, "For those who are led by the Spirit of God are the children of God. The Spirit you received does not make you slaves, so that you live in fear again; rather, the Spirit you received brought about your adoption to sonship. And by him we cry, "*Abba,* Father." The Spirit himself testifies with our spirit that we are God's children. Now if we are children, then we are heirs—heirs of God and coheirs with Christ, if indeed we share in his sufferings in order that we may also share in his glory" (Rom. 8:14-17 NIV). So what is so good about the good news? The good news is that God adopted us. Adoption comes from a word that reflects a Roman system. In this system it gave the father absolute authority. He had "patria potestas." It is a Latin phrase meaning power of the father. Under Roman law, the father had absolute power over his family, including the power of life and death. When a child was born, and the father did not want the child, he would abandon the infant outside, to be exposed to the weather, which, depending on the time of the year, may kill the child within a few hours. In fact, the early church took to heart the biblical instruction about caring for orphans in their distress (James 1:27) and began to take in the abandoned babies from around the city—a large number of which were girls because every Roman father wanted a son to whom he would pass on his inheritance.

But please don't think that all Roman fathers were so callous and heartless. Most female babies were raised in their own homes by their natural parents, but among those babies who were abandoned, virtually all of them were females or were deformed in some way. Roman fathers had the absolute power of disposal and control within their family, and absolutely no recourse could be taken against him.

Also, in regard to his father, a Roman son never came to age. No matter how old he was, he was still under patria potestas, as were the daughters. No matter how old they were, they were still under the absolute control of the father. This made adoption into a family a very difficult and very serious matter unless the person was an illegitimate child or an orphan, because Roman law provided that a man could adopt the son of another man only if the natural father agreed to allow that to occur. And because the father maintained his *patria potestas* over his son for life, he could give up his son for adoption at any age—even well into adulthood.

In the first century, when Paul was writing this, adopted children were, in many cases, more honored than natural children. In virtually all cases, it was seen as an act of honor to be adopted, because that child—who was born into a world filled with illegitimate children and orphaned children—could say, "I was chosen by someone. I wasn't just born into a family where what you get is what you get . . . I was chosen."

So being adopted was a noble thing. An adopted son was deliberately chosen by the adopting father to perpetuate that father's name and to inherit that father's estate. And when a father in the Roman world didn't have a son, he would go find the noblest available son and adopt him and give him all the rights and privileges of a natural-born son.

The adopted son was in no way inferior. In fact, he may have been chosen because he was deemed to be superior to the natural-born son. Many Roman fathers had sons who, in their eyes, didn't measure up to their qualifications to inherit their estate, so they went out and found one that did. So an adopted son may have received more affection from his father than a naturally born son, and he may well have represented his father's moral standards more perfectly than that man's natural sons. And that's the whole point of biblical adoption, which is that we become children of God by sovereign divine choice. We are the preferred choice of God. On the basis of free and voluntary election, God has chosen us to be adopted as His sons. We will never be condemned because God has chosen us to be His children forever by His free grace and His uninfluenced sovereignty. He will never disinherit us. We have been lifted to this place of honor, and He will fulfill in us His good purposes.

The reason for man's adoption is because God wanted mankind to become His children. But man lost some things when he sinned in the Garden of Eden. Ever since the first sin, man has been birthed in sin and shaped in inequity and thus belongs to the family of Satan. But in order to get into the family of God there had to be a legal document, and that is where the cross at Calvary became significant in a Christian's life. Christ had to die on the cross in order to pay the price so that man could be pulled out of Satan's family and transplanted into the family of God. Therefore we became sons and daughters of the Lord.

There are only sixteen times in the Old Testament where God was called Father. The sixteen times that He was called Father it was never meant to mean a personal or interpersonal Father. God was always looked at as being a Father of a nation. They would use the name Yaweh rather than Father. So, when Jesus came onto the scene calling God Father, it was a new and revolutionary break with Jewish sayings and customs. But Jesus said, "When you pray say abba Father." It was a term of endearment and a term of closeness. He basically called Him "daddy." According to Jewish religious tradition, you are blaspheming God's name by calling Him daddy. Jesus was informing those who accept his death and resurrection that they are adopted into God's family. But when God becomes your daddy he does daddy kind of things. He not only provides for you, but he also disciplines you. He will bless you but holds you accountable as well. If a man or woman can sin and there is no remorse by them for what they've done, then perhaps they need to check and see if they've been adopted by the Father. But if you are part of God's family and you disobey Him, he will chastise you. It is just like the model He set up in our family household. You cannot rebel against your daddy without him implementing some kind of discipline in your life. The New Testament uses the imagery of adoption to illustrate what has happened to us in salvation. To be born into God's family is a special thing. But to say that out of all the people in the world, God Himself chose you, wiped away the record of all of your sin, and gave you full status as a son and joint heir with His Son Jesus Christ is beyond our ability to express.

 4

The Good News of Our Redemption

"Non-Christians seem to think that the Incarnation implies some particular merit or excellence in humanity. But of course it implies just the reverse: a particular demerit and depravity. No creature that deserved Redemption would need to be redeemed. They that are whole need not the physician. Christ died for men precisely because men are not worth dying for; to make them worth it."

C. S. Lewis (1898-1963)

R edemption means to recover something that you once owned but is now in the possession of someone else. It also means to "buy out." In order to get that which was once owned by you, there must be a pledge, contract, or payment in order to get it back. Genesis chapter 3 is the first account of man losing its possession. Adam sinned and lost the immortality of his body and the inheritance of the earth. That is why we have sickness in our bodies and struggles in our experiences. Adam was no longer the dominant figure on the earth. The inheritance of earth was then passed over to the possession of Satan. However, the Levitical law found in Leviticus 25 allows a kinsman redeemer to buy back a lost possession. Jesus was a kinsman to Adam and bought back man's inheritance and immortality. Of all the names that the Bible gives and of all the names that believers give to Jesus Christ, none is more precious than the name Redeemer. There are other names we use more often, such as Lord and Savior, and rightly so because those too are Bible terms, but no word touches the heart like the word redeemer. When we say Lord, we are recalling that Jesus Christ is the master over sin and death. When we say Savior, we are recalling that he saved us from our sin. But when we say Redeemer, we remember what it cost him to save us. Redeemer is the name of Christ on the cross. When we say that word, the cross is placed before our eyes. We remember not only that he gave us salvation, but that he paid a mighty price for it.

Three Greek words are used in the New Testament for redemption. The first is *agorazo*. It comes from the Greek *agora*, which means the marketplace. In its secular sense, it means to go into the marketplace and buy something. You see something you like and purchase it. Applied to redemption, it means to go in and purchase a slave who is on the auction block.

The second word is *exagorazo*. *Ex* means out of. When you add it to *agorazo* it means to go into the slave market, to pay the price, and to take somebody off the slave market and out of that area altogether.

The third word is the word *lutron*, which means to set free or deliver somebody from captivity. Now then, *agorazo* means to purchase; *exagorazo* means to purchase and remove from the slave market; *lutron* means having purchased and removed—you are now set free.

All three words are used in the New Testament to describe what Jesus did on the cross. Ephesians 1:7 says, "In him we have redemption through his blood, the forgiveness of sins, in accordance with the riches of God's grace." Titus 2:14 says, "Who gave himself for us to redeem us from all wickedness." Galatians 3:13 says, "Christ redeemed us from the curse of the law." 1 Peter 1:18-19 says, "For you know that it was not with perishable things such as silver or gold that you were redeemed from the empty way of life handed down to you from your forefathers, but with the precious blood of Christ, a lamb without blemish or defect." Instead of our death, there is His death. Instead of our blood, there is His blood.

Many years ago, the local grocery stores gave their customers trading stamps as a bonus for purchasing groceries from them. One particular scheme gave one stamp for every ten cents worth of groceries purchased. They called them "redemption stamps." Customers who purchased a large amount of groceries could expect to accumulate enough stamps to earn valuable rewards. They pasted the stamps into stamp books, and took them to a "redemption center" to cash in on merchandise—dishes, appliances, or any number of items from a catalog. Today, there are few such redemption centers in existence. Even if you possess great quantities of trading stamps, they are worthless without a redeemer. The same is true about our souls. If it were not for Jesus Christ our Redeemer, our souls would have no value. Only Jesus can give us value and reward in exchange for our sinful souls. The act of redemption is like the act of paying ransom for a hostage. Criminals often kidnap a person with the intention of extorting a reward or expending him or her for some tragic purpose. It is an act of felony. Unless a ransom is paid, the hostage's life is in real jeopardy. That is essentially what Satan did in the Garden of Eden. He took Adam and Eve captive at his will (see 2 Tim. 2:26). Unless God is willing to pay our ransom, we will not be saved. We will perish under the curse of our sins, because the wages of sin is death. Redemption saves us from sin and its consequences. Redemption makes up for the tragic losses due to sin. Redemption restores the honor, worth, and reputation of its victim. This is what God does for us.

R. C. Sproul said, "God just doesn't throw a life preserver to a drowning person. He goes to the bottom of the sea, and pulls a corpse from the bottom of the sea, takes him up on the bank, breathes into him the breath of life and makes him alive. That is what the Bible says happens in your salvation."

Practically everyone loves a good redemption story. It's part of our human nature to cheer when the fallen get back up and become the victors. Hollywood is full of movies and stories of characters that were broken, fallen, or rejected, but they got a second chance and rose to be the hero, the lover, and everybody's favorite person. Although, we all love a redemption story when it's all finished, and we love people who have been through tough things and are telling the stories now that they're all cleaned up, healed up, and on the other side. Somehow we are not good at loving people who are still broken or are in the process of getting restored. The good news is Jesus loves redemption from beginning to end. God is not intimidated by our brokenness. He loves the long, slow process of taking the broken, softening them up, and remaking them into the beautiful. He loves just holding broken pieces in His hand—dreaming of what they'll look like if they'll just let Him take and form them and make them new. He loves treating broken pieces with all the love and care of a finished masterpiece.

In recent years used cars have started to post warnings to customers in big letters that advise that a pre-owned vehicle is being sold with no warranty, so the buyer should beware that the purchase price does not include a return, repair, or any other consideration; it is being sold "as is." "As is" does not always mean that the product is bad, but it does always mean that no warranty is attached to it. Anyone who purchases it does so with the full knowledge that once he or she gets home there is a possibility that the purchase may disappoint him or her. That doesn't disappoint a person who has a restoration in mind. The young man who buys an old car that is dented, inoperable, and ugly knows that he's probably buying a lemon, but he has restoration in mind. He's planning to remove the dents, give it a new paint job, give it some new wheels, spruce up the interior, and add a few hydraulics. He buys the old car "as is," but he has something else in mind.

God had something of this nature in mind when he looked down on this world and saw its sad condition and decided to redeem it to himself. What he saw was a world filled with sin, hate, and ungodliness. Yet he loved the world so much that he gave his only begotten son, who purchased our salvation with his own blood. What he purchased was a real wreck, but what he had in mind was restoration. As Christians, we should rejoice that our God looked down on our feeble condition and loved us enough to look beyond our immediate faults and flaws and see our needs. We came to him in a state of "as is," but when God gets through with us we shall come forth as pure gold.

The reason that He accepts us is because He sees what we can be. Just as your beautician sees the final design of your hair, the doctor sees your health after your surgery, and the teacher sees your life after graduation, God sees what you can be when He gets through with you. He sees what we can be, but to get us there He may find it necessary to take us apart, strip us down, so He can put us back together again. He told the prophet Jeremiah to go the potter's house and watch the potter work. As the potter worked with the clay, when he found a flaw he tore down the whole creation and started over again. God told Jeremiah that is what he has to do to His people sometimes: tear them down to build them up again. First Corinthians 2:9 says, "Eye hath not seen, nor ear heard, neither have entered into the heart of man, the things which God hath prepared for them that love him" (KJV). God is working with us. We are not there yet. That's why the song writer wrote, "Please be patient with me. God is not through with me yet. When God gets through, I shall come forth as pure gold."

We must remember that when Jesus purchased our salvation He paid a high price for damaged merchandise. Whenever a person purchases an item, he expects a discount if the item has been used, broken, or damaged in some way. Very few people would pay the retail price for "as is" merchandise.

Yet, when God looked down on the world He decided to redeem it for Himself, but that redemption would not be discounted. His word remained unchanged. Romans 6:23 says, "For the wages of sin is death, but the gift of God is eternal life." How does a sinful person like me come before God? There is only one way to come, and that's to come "as is." That is what Charlotte Elliott learned many years ago when she was visiting friends and met a preacher at a dinner who asked her if she was a Christian. She was offended by the question, but it would not go away. Weeks later she met the same preacher again and told him that his question troubled her, but she did not know how to find Him, and neither did she feel worthy. The preacher told her that God is always nearby, and to "just come to him as you are." She accepted Christ that day and later wrote a song that said, "Just as I am without one plea, but that thy blood was shed for me; and that thou bidst me come to thee, O Lamb of God, I come, I come."

 **5**

The Good News of Our Forgiveness

"Forgiveness is the remission of sins. For it is by this that what has been lost, and was found, is saved from being lost again."

Augustine (254-430 AD)

I n Ephesians 1:7 Paul says, "In him we have redemption through his blood, the forgiveness of sins, in accordance with the riches of God's grace." There is good news about our forgiveness. To forgive means to release others from a debt incurred when they wronged us. The debt may be material or emotional, some form of hurt or embarrassment. We cannot be right with God and unforgiving toward others. Confession is absolutely essential if we are to walk in fellowship with our heavenly Father, whose forgiveness toward us is eternal. When we fully comprehend God's forgiveness toward us, we simply cannot justify our holding anyone else accountable. Because Christ dwells in us as believers, we have a spiritual nature to forgive. As we forgive one another, we release ourselves from bitterness. Emotional release enables physical and spiritual healing, and it frees us from bondage to other people. As we forgive one another, we enjoy reconciliation and the joy of healthy, loving relationships. Forgiveness is an accompanying word with redemption. The two words work hand and hand. You cannot have redemption without forgiveness.

In Hebrew, the dominant word in the Old Testament that is translated as forgiveness is *nasa/nasah*. It means "to lift," as in, "to lift someone's punishment from off of him." Similarly, in the New Testament the most often used Greek word translated as forgive is *aphiemi*. It means "to send away," as if to say, "to send away someone's punishment."

One who is forgiven in the Bible is released from his duly "earned" punishments or obligations of restitution. The first instance of the word *forgive (nasa/nasah:* to send away a person's punishment) is found in Genesis 50:17. Joseph's brothers begged him to forgive them and to not bear a "grudge against us and pay us back in full for all the wrong which we did" (Gen. 50:15-17). Notice the circumstances. His brothers really were guilty of doing him wrong; they acknowledged their guilt, and they knew they had never been fully punished ("paid back") for the evil actions they performed. They wanted Joseph to forgive this moral debt entirely, to take no further punitive actions, and to release them from the just penalty that they deserved. Joseph took the action of absolving them, agreeing to impose no further punishment. The New Testament scriptures sums this up in 1 John 1:8-9, "If we claim to be without sin, we deceive ourselves and the truth is not in us. If we confess our sins, he is faithful and just and will forgive us our sins and purify us from all unrighteousness" (NIV).

God hates sin, and the requirements for forgiveness are high. One requirement is sacrifice. Hebrews 9:22 says that "without the shedding of Blood, there is no forgiveness." In the Old Testament, a sacrifice of an unblemished lamb was required to satisfy God's wrath. Jesus, the sinless Son of God, died on the cross and became the ultimate sacrifice for sin. Jesus bought our forgiveness when He died on the cross. Another requirement for forgiveness of sins is that we forgive others. First Corinthians 13:5 says that "real love keeps no record of wrongs." Remember that Proverbs 17:9 tells us that a real friend will forgive. God has also made forgiving others a requirement for receiving His forgiveness. We must confess our sins to God if our relationship with Him is to be restored completely. Looking back at the real need for forgiveness, we see that unconfessed sin can separate us in our relationship with God. Confession is the way to restore that relationship with the Lord, remembering that it is for our own benefit that we confess to return to the Lord because He is faithful even when we are not (2 Tim. 2:13). Lastly, we must repent. We must decide to change, to turn from our sins. Jeremiah states in 15:19, "Therefore this is what the Lord says, If you repent, I will restore you that you may serve me".

Genesis chapter 3 records the fall of man. He fell in numerous ways. He fell physically and spiritually. Prior to the fall Adam had an expansive mind and vocabulary. He knew all of the animals in the world. He named everything and had dominion over the earth. He fell physically when he sinned and lost the immortality of his body. His physical death did not happen for quite some time because of the longevity of life at that time. However his spiritual death occurred immediately. He was alienated from God and began to hide behind trees to avoid Him. As a result of this, Adam and his seed were eternally banished and separated from God. But man's sin did not surprise God. Before He created man He had already provided redemption and forgiveness. He was going to do a greater work through redemption than He did in Creation.

It is important for mankind to accept Jesus as their personal Savior to not be continually separated and alienated from God.

You may have a college education and much of the world's acquisitions, but if you have not accepted Jesus then you're still separated from God. Education can refine human nature, but it cannot change it. You must have the power of God that comes through Christ in order to change your inner life. That is why a man must be regenerated. Regeneration means to be born again. It is the spiritual change brought about in the heart of man by the Holy Spirit in which his or her inherently sinful nature is changed so that he or she can respond to God in faith. I thank God for the laws of this land, but laws will not make men and women love one another. Laws will make men and women sit shoulder to shoulder but it takes the Lord to put you together heart to heart.

Forgiveness is a powerful and profound concept that lies at the very heart of the Christian message. Our God is a forgiving God. We are forgiven people. We, in turn, have been called to forgive others. What does it mean to truly forgive?

Here are some things it doesn't mean:

1. Forgiveness is not kissing and making up and pretending nothing ever happened.

2. Forgiveness is not repressing feelings or avoiding hard truths for the sake of surface harmony.

3. Forgiveness is not a get-out-jail-free card that sidesteps consequences and circumvents the need for true penitence.

4. Forgiveness is not trying to put the toothpaste back into the tube, restoring everything back to the way it was prior to the offense.

Godly forgiveness involves:

1. Cleansing the heart of anger, resentment, and hatred toward those who have offended us.

2. Growing to the point where we can pray for those who have hurt us and can bless rather than curse them.

3. A willingness to overcome personal heartache in order to rebuild trust where true penitence and sorrow for sin are demonstrably present.

4. An openness to reconciliation, if trust can be reestablished.

At the most basic level, forgiveness is about what goes on inside our hearts. It's anger control, resentment purging, bitterness cleansing. At this level, it doesn't really matter if the people we forgive are repentant—if they actually "get" what they have done and how they have wounded. This kind of forgiveness is about who we are and the state of our own hearts, not who the offender is and whether he or she is sorry for what was done.

During World War II, as Allied soldiers fought their way across France, a soldier died during a bloody firefight. After the battle was over, his buddies wanted to find a way to give him a decent burial. The only cemetery in the closest village was a Catholic cemetery, so they approached the priest, asking for permission to bury their fallen comrade there. "Is he Catholic?" the priest asked. "No, he's Protestant," came the reply. With great regret, the priest said, "He cannot be buried here. This cemetery is reserved for baptized members of the Catholic Church." So the soldiers found a suitable place outside the fence that marked the border of the cemetery. With great sorrow, they buried him and then went back to the war. Some months later, the soldiers returned to the tiny village, hoping to provide a suitable marker for their friend. To their surprise and consternation, when they came to the burial spot, they could not find the grave. Not knowing what else to do, they asked the priest if he knew what had happened. He told them that after they had buried their friend; he could not sleep at night. So one morning he got up early and moved the fence to include the body of the much-loved soldier who had died for his country.

That's what God did for us. He could not rest while we're on the wrong side of the fence. He wanted so much to bring us into his family that he sent his Son, the Lord Jesus Christ, who through his death on the cross "moved the fence" so that we would have a place in God's family.

If God has "moved the fence" for us, can we not do the same for others? If God found a way to include us in his love, can we not reach out to include those who have sinned against us? This is the very heart of the gospel. What God has freely done for us, we are called to do for others. The heart of God is filled with love, and at its center stands a cross. Through that cross we have been forgiven. May God give us grace to "move the fence" for others as God has "moved the fence" for us.

6

The Good News of Atonement

"Your sins indeed are great, but by baptism I [i.e., Christ] bestow on you my righteousness; I strip death from you and clothe you with my life. That's Christ's true regimen; his office and mission are summed up in this, that he daily strips away our sin and death and clothes us with his righteousness and life."

(Martin Luther 1483-1546)

T he word "atonement" means just what it says, at-one-ment. The Hebrew word for atonement is *kaphar,* which means to cover. The verb form is found seventy-one times in the Old Testament. The noun form is found nine times. The English word "atonement" occurs only once in the New Testament (Rom. 5:11). The Greek word for atonement is *katallage*, which means to reconcile.

The idea behind atonement is to make two as one. It means to reconcile a difference or to remove a separation between two persons. It can mean settling differences between a wife and a husband (2 Cor. 7:11), the cleansing of lepers (Lev. 14), the cleansing of the house of God (Ezek. 45:17, 20), and many other instances. But the majority of instances refer to a reconciliation between God and man (Exod. 29:36-37, Rom. 5:10-11, and 2 Cor. 5:20).

God created man for His fellowship (Gen. 2:7, 3:8; Rom. 5:11), but sin separated them (Isa. 59:2). Man was expelled from the physical presence of God as a result of his sin in the Garden of Eden. The perfect fellowship between God and man had to be restored through atonement.

The Hebrew Day of Atonement (Lev. 23:27-28), also known as Yom Kippur, was the most solemn holy day of all the Israelite feasts and festivals, occurring once a year on the tenth day of Tishri, the seventh month of the Hebrew calendar. On that day, the high priest performed elaborate rituals to atone for the sins of the people. In Leviticus 16:1-34, the atonement ritual began with Aaron, or subsequent high priests of Israel, coming into the holy of holies. The solemnity of the day was underscored by God telling Moses to warn Aaron not to come into the Most Holy Place whenever he felt like it, only on this special day once a year, lest he die (v. 2). This was not a ceremony to be taken lightly, and the people were to understand that atonement for sin was to be done God's way.

Before entering, Aaron was to bathe and put on special garments (v. 4), then sacrifice a bull for a sin offering for himself and his family (vv. 6, 11). The blood of the bull was to be sprinkled on the Ark of the Covenant. Then he was to bring two goats, one to be sacrificed "because of the uncleanness and rebellion of the Israelites, whatever their sins have been" (v. 16), and its blood was sprinkled on the ark. The other goat was used as a scapegoat. Aaron placed his hands on its head, confessed over it the rebellion and wickedness of the Israelites, and sent the goat out with an appointed man, who released it into the wilderness (v. 21). The goat carried on itself all the sins of the people, which were forgiven for another year (v. 30).

Under the Old Covenant, or Testament, there were annual days of atonement; under the New Covenant there is but one. For Jews, who rejected Jesus as their Messiah, animal sacrifices were stopped in AD 70 when Jerusalem and the temple were destroyed by the Romans. Jesus predicted this in the Gospels. For Christians, animal sacrifices stopped with the death and resurrection of Jesus. Man was hungry for fellowship with God but was unable to heal the breach (Rom.

1-3). The issue was now up to God. To Him the problem was how to remain just and yet be the justifier. Since the "wages of sin is death," only by death could the breach be healed. The one dying must be sinless (Exod. 32:32; lamb without spot or blemish; 1 Pet. 1:19). Therefore it became God's duty to pay the price in the incarnation of Himself in Jesus (John 1: 14, 29; Heb. 9:14).

The atonement involves both priest and sacrifice. Jesus is both. In His life, death, resurrection, and continuing ministry in heaven, Jesus Christ fulfilled (gave full meaning to) every ministry of the tabernacle or temple, both on the Day of Atonement and beyond. Thus, the fellowship between God and man has been restored. When Jesus died on the cross, the veil of the temple was torn in two from top to bottom (Matt. 27:51), enabling us to "come boldly unto the throne of grace, that we may obtain mercy, and find grace to help in a time of need."

This is in no way an exhaustive look at this great doctrine, but hopefully is enough to whet the appetite of Christians of the cross, who desire to understand how God is just and the Justifier. All believers from Adam to the end of time have been atoned for at the same time—at the cross. That is where all our sins are put away, and God declared them righteous (just). Even by Adam's one disobedience we were all made sinners, so by the righteousness of one (Christ) we have been declared righteous, acquitted of all guilt.

7

The Good News of Evangelism

"Evangelism is just one beggar telling another beggar where to find bread."

D. T. Niles (1908-70)

I t is rather ironic that the word evangelism comes from the Greek word euangelion, meaning a messenger bringing good news. It renders the same definition as the word gospel in chapter 1. For Christians, the two words work together. High on God's "to-do list" is the evangelization of His people. Matthew 28:18-20 says, "Then Jesus came to them and said, "All authority in heaven and on earth has been given to me. Therefore go and make disciples of all nations, baptizing them in the name of the Father and of the Son and of the Holy Spirit, and teaching them to obey everything I have commanded you. And surely I am with you always, to the very end of the age."

Have you ever shared good news with anyone? Were you ever excited to tell someone about a really good movie you saw? Most of us have had that experience and were really anxious to tell someone about it. But why do most Christians panic when the thought of sharing Jesus with others goes through their minds?

In his book *Lifestyle Evangelism: Learning to Open Your Life to Those around You*, Joseph Aldrich writes that there is a legend recounting the return of Jesus to glory after his time on earth. Even in heaven He bore the marks of His earthly pilgrimage—with His cruel cross and shameful death. The angel Gabriel approached Him and said, "Master, you must have suffered terribly for men down there." "I did," He said. "Do they all know about how you love them and what you did for them?" "Oh no," said Jesus, "not yet. Right now only a handful of people in Palestine know." Gabriel was perplexed. "Then, what have you done," he asked, "to let everyone know about your love for them?" Jesus said, "I've asked Peter, James, and John, and a few more friends, to tell other people about me. Those who were told will in turn tell other people about me and my story will spread to the furthest reaches of the globe. Ultimately, all of mankind will have heard about my life, and what I have done." Gabriel frowned and looked rather skeptical. He knew well what poor stuff men are made of. "Yes," he said, "but what if Peter, James, and John grow weary? What if the people who come after them forget? What if in the twentieth century people just don't tell others about you? Haven't you made any other plans?" Jesus answered, "I haven't made any other plans. I'm counting on them."

Twenty centuries later He still has no other plan. He's counting on you and me. Christ counted on His disciples, and they delivered. How well will we deliver? If I could write Joseph Aldrich's story from that point I would have to say that this generation has dropped the baton.

Chuck Swindoll gives four attitudes that hinder the progress of the gospel. The first attitude is the attitude of specialization. Quoting from the old television program *Chico and the Man*, we often say, "That's not my job!" We believe that the work of evangelism is to be done by someone who specializes in it, much like a cardiologist who specializes in heart surgery.

The second attitude Swindoll gives us is the attitude of isolation. It comes from the incorrect answer to the biblical question found in Genesis 4:9 when God asks Cain where his brother Abel is. Cain replied, "Am I my brother's keeper?" We believe that the world is too big for us to take on the burden of sharing the gospel to so many people. Thus, we tend to our own business and concerns. Mother Teresa was asked how she planned to feed all of the people in India who were starving and dying of malnutrition. She answered, "One at a time."

The third attitude is procrastination. A poet gave this illustration: A farm boy accidentally overturned his wagonload of corn in the road. The farmer who lived nearby came to investigate. "Hey, Willis," he called out. "Forget your troubles for a spell and come on in and have dinner with us, and then I'll help you get the wagon up." "That's mighty nice of you," Willis answered, "But I don't think Papa would like me to." "Aw, come on, son!" the farmer insisted. "Well, okay," the boy finally agreed. "But Papa won't like it." After a hearty dinner, Willis thanked his host. "I feel a lot better now, but I just know Papa is going to be real upset." "Don't be foolish!" exclaimed the neighbor. "By the way, where is he?" The farm boy replied, "He's under the wagon." Certain things in life cannot be put off to a later time. Accepting Christ as our Savior should be the number one priority in our spiritual journey; telling others about Him should be the number two priority! Yet, we give a multitude of excuses why we don't share the saving grace of Christ with others. It becomes a matter of priority.

The fourth attitude is rejection. Rejection is when Christians give all they can to win souls for Christ but are often rejected by those they encounter. John R. Stotts describes such a person as a "rabbit Christian." It is a Christian who peeks his head up in the morning and leaves his Christian classmates as he scurries off to class while hoping to find a seat next to another Christian. We do this because we are intimidated by the hostility that the world demonstrated toward Christ and His followers. Church-going becomes a matter of a "good exercise." Christians do not want to be criticized when it comes to sharing the gospel of Jesus.

The message of the gospel appears to be foolishness. When it comes to spiritual matters we lend too much respect to the intellectuals of our society. We do not want the philosophers and scholars of the world to think that we are foolish because of our belief in the gospel. Many believe that the message of the gospel is weak, irrelevant, and intellectual foolishness. In a subtle way it is foolishness from a human horizontal perspective. The Bible states that if you want to go up, you have to first go down. If you want to live, then you have to die. If you want to have things, you have to give everything away. Logically, it is preposterous to think that Jesus died on a cross two thousand years ago so that men and women could be saved. If you think of it on a horizontal level then it is a foolish phenomenon. But one must also have a vertical or heavenly perspective on life. If we are the beneficiaries of Christ's blood, then we should not mind being bearers of His cross and proclaimers of his purpose.

Jesus states in Matthew 28:18 that "all authority in heaven and on earth is given to me." The word "authority" in the original Greek language is *exousia*. He has taken his *exousia* (authority) and given that also to His *ekklesia* (church). But what does it mean for the church of Jesus Christ to have all authority in heaven and on earth behind it? Jesus wanted to make sure that His church will be empowered to do whatever imperative, mandate, mission, or commission He assigns them to do. Therefore, all excuses concerning evangelism are obliterated.

One example of God's power demonstrated through His people is found in Acts 3:1-3. Peter and John were on their way to the temple to pray. Sitting outside the temple was a lame beggar who was asking for alms. Peter responded, "Sir, I apologize because we don't have any silver or gold. We're just two broke preachers on our way to prayer meeting. But, I'll give you what I have." The lame man replied, "Give me some of what you have." Peter then began to direct divine authority *(paraphrased)*. I can imagine Peter praying, saying, "Jesus, Son of the Father. I've got a man here who has a congenital birth defect. He needs some help, Lord, and he needs it now. Lord, I know you can put your power anywhere you want it, but I need your power on this particular spot." Peter called the name of Jesus Christ of Nazareth, and God released His power from the "coast of glory." Someone once said that power came quicker than right now and sooner than at once. Peter took the man by his right hand, and the power hit this lame man in the mole of his head and ran down to the soles of his feet. Luke, the physician tells us in the original language what was wrong with the man's foot. He said his anklebone was dislocated from his foot bone. Therefore his leg had no control over his foot. But when the power of God hit the lame man it welded the foot bone to the leg bone. Not only did the man start walking, but he also started leaping and praising God. This miracle was done because Peter exercised the authority that was given to him by God. Never underestimate the power of prayer.

In Matthew 28: 18-20, Jesus gives us the imperative, and that is to make disciples. Surrounding the imperative are three participles—go, baptize, and teach. When there is an imperative in interpretive scripture that is surrounded by three participles, the imperative describes the mandate while the participle describes the methodology. In other words, the imperative tells us what our task is. In this text the imperative is to make disciples. How do we make disciples? It is found in the methods go, baptize, and teach. Christians have been called by the Lord to make disciples and not be decision makers, conformers or just churchgoers. General William Booth, the founder of the Salvation Army, was invited to visit Buckingham Palace. He wrote in an autographed album that some men's ambition is art, some men's ambition is fame, and some men's ambition is gold, but his ambition was to see the souls of men come to Christ. Here is a man obsessed with seeing the souls of men come to Christ. Proverbs 11:30 says, "He that winneth souls is wise" (KJV). If you turn that statement around it would say, "He that does not winneth souls is not wise."

Evangelism is not just a suggestion from Jesus but a mandate. We often allow the activity of the organization to eclipse our vision of the activity of the organism. We become so consumed in church work until we lose sight of the work of the church. The main thing is to make disciples, and to make sure that the main thing becomes no less than the main thing. Jesus says in Matthew 4:19, "Follow me, and I will make you fishers of men." If you're not fishing, then you are not following. If you follow Jesus, then He will make a fisher of men out of you.

During the Memorial Day weekend of 2007, my wife and I had the pleasure of going on a short-term mission trip to Baja California, Mexico. Each year many families across the United States and Canada meet in San Diego to travel together across the border to serve in Mexico by building homes for families in need. Each home is built by a family mission team made up of approximately twenty-five individuals. It was a unique experience to serve side by side with my wife in a spiritual and relevant way. This experience was in many ways the most important experience of my spiritual life. When I was immersed in the culture of a broken, wounded, and completely unpretentious people, it forced me to let go of my relevant self. The self that could do things, show things, prove things, and articulate things in meaningful ways no longer mattered. God had now placed me in an environment where I was to receive and give love regardless of my accomplishments. I say this because I am convinced that the Christian leaders of the future are called to be completely irrelevant. They are to stand forth in this world with nothing to offer but his or her own vulnerable self. The message we have to carry, as ministers of God's word, is that God loves us not because of what we do or accomplish. Instead, we are to be selfless—to die to self and to deflect any attention given to us to the great God who created and sustains us.

Jesus's first temptation was to turn stones into bread. It would have been awesome for me to do that in Mexico. As we drove down the dusty streets of the little shantytown on the outskirts of Tijuana, Mexico, where children die from malnutrition and contaminated water, it would have been nice to turn the rocks on the street into donuts, coffee cakes, or freshly baked bread. It would have been nice to turn the stale drinking water that we used to mix the concrete into delicious milk. Aren't we Christians who are called to heal the sick, feed the hungry, and ease the suffering of the poor? It didn't take us long to learn on our mission trip that you not only serve those in need, but you will in turn leave this experience changed. It was a culture without certainties. Maybe there would be food tomorrow; maybe there would be work tomorrow; maybe there would be happiness tomorrow—maybe or maybe not. The word most often heard and said was *gracias* (thank you). Food, clothing, shelter, and work are all given to us by the grace of God. Why? So that we can say *gracias*, thanks to God and thanks to each other. We finished our house for the family of six people in four days. They could not pay us for building their new home, but what they gave us was a smile and the word *gracias*. In four days we built relationships and closeness. Tears rolled down our eyes as we drove away from our assigned family. In just a few days our hands contributed to helping transform a family's life forever. But most of all I will not forget the transformation it made in my own life! For that I say, *"Gracias, Dios"* (thank you, God).

The Good News of Soteriology: Saved from What to What

"The thief had nails through both hands, so that he could not work; and a nail through each foot, so that he could not run errands for the Lord; he could not lift a hand or a foot toward his salvation, and yet Christ offered him the gift of God; and he took it. Christ threw him a passport, and took him into Paradise."

Dwight L. Moody (1837-99)

S oteriology is the study of the doctrine of salvation. It is a noun that comes from the Greek verb that in the Septuagint is used to translate words meaning to save, to keep safe and sound, and to rescue from danger or destruction. It is the opposite of *appollumi*, meaning to destroy, from which we get the name Apollyon, one of the names of Satan (Rev. 9:11). In the New Testament it is sometimes used in the same sense of saving or rescuing from danger or destruction (Matt. 8:25; Acts 27:20, 31; 2 Pet. 4:18). It also refers to healing (Matt. 9:22), both physical and spiritual (Luke 7:50). The greatest use of this verb is to mean deliverance from the messianic judgment (Joel 2:32), to save from the evils that obstruct the messianic deliverance (Matt. 1:21, Rom. 5:9, James 5:20), to make one a partaker of the salvation offered by Christ (Matt. 19:25, John 3:17) (Bauer, 1979). The Greek word *soterios* refers to the one bringing salvation (Titus 2:11, Luke 2:30, 3:6, Acts 28:28).

Salvation begins with the admission that there is nothing good in us, that nothing in us can contribute to our salvation, that we are utterly helpless and unable to save ourselves, and that salvation must come from outside of us. We must confess that we need the help that only Jesus can supply.

God offers salvation on one simple and single condition—a wholehearted faith in Jesus Christ—trusting Him alone as Lord and Savior, resting upon Him for complete salvation, renouncing all self-trust, admitting our sinfulness, confessing our need, and crying out to Jesus to save us from our sins.

Those who trust in Jesus Christ and him alone are saved forever. They are forgiven of all their sins, born again, brought into God's family, and declared righteous while they were still sinners. Their sins are placed on Christ, and his righteousness is imputed to them, and they receive a new nature that enables them to walk in a brand-new direction. They are given eternal life and guaranteed they will go to heaven when they die. This is what John 3:16 means when it says that "God so loved the world." This is the good news Jesus told us to preach "to all creation" (Mark 16:15).

Why do we need this message? Because no one can be good enough! No one can work hard enough! No one can do anything to merit a place in heaven! The great danger we humans face is that we will change the gospel message into a "Christ plus" religion. Some are told to believe in Jesus, but then we add in good works, baptism, the Mass, the sacraments, giving, and church attendance as part of what God requires for us to go to heaven. Those things come as a result of being saved. Paul taught "all of Christ and none of me." If we teach "some of Christ and some of me" we are not teaching a biblical gospel.

Perhaps one of the reasons we are not enthusiastic about our salvation is because we do not know what we have been saved from, and we do not know what we have been saved to.

A group of Africans were in Africa playing marbles with diamonds. They had smoothed out the edges of the diamonds and were having fun playing marbles. An Englishman appeared before them and said, "I'd like a set of those marbles." The Africans replied, "You like to shoot marbles?" The Englishman said, "Oh yes, I love to shoot marbles, but I want to be fair with you and give you something in return." The Englishman reached into his bag and gave them a bottle of whiskey. The Englishman returned to England with five million dollars' worth of diamonds for a bottle of whiskey! When you don't know what you have and the value of what you have, you will rejoice about the wrong things.

Theologically the word "saved" does not mean physical perfection, nor does it mean spiritual perfection because we all have physical afflictions and spiritual imperfections. But God has arranged a substitute for us, and we must accept the substitute. In the game of baseball you can substitute one player for another player. The only thing you have to do when being substituted is to "step aside." The batter that was going to bat doesn't have to do anything but "step aside." This illustration is much like our relationship with God. We do not have to argue our case for salvation with God because we have stepped aside and allowed Jesus to step up and argue our case. Acts 16:31 tells you to "believe in the Lord Jesus, and you will be saved—you and your household." You are, therefore, covered by the blood of the Lamb that was settled on Calvary. Therefore you are covered if you have accepted Jesus Christ as your Lord and Savior. But that is our position and not our condition. We are saved by our position, but our condition often yields to the ways of the flesh. The Holy Spirit is constantly working on our condition. Every now and then the Spirit tosses something out such as a bad habit. But one great morning when this life is over, He shall present us faultless, without a spot and without a wrinkle. But in the meantime you're covered.

A little girl walked up to a man on a street corner and said, "Sir, have you been saved?" The man looked down at her with a smile, and he said, "Yes, young lady, I have been saved. But beyond that, I am being saved, and one day I will be saved." That man knew what he was talking about. Unfortunately, we commonly regard salvation in one sense only, and that is redemption from sin. But a careful examination of the use of the word and its equivalents will reveal that salvation in a spiritual sense is used to express three different ideas. As a Christian I have been saved from the penalty of sin. I am being saved from the power of sin. One day I will be saved from the wrath to come.

The saved are saved from the penalty of sin. Roman 8:1 states, "Therefore, there is now no condemnation for those who are in Christ Jesus." We were born in sin; therefore, we were born penalized. The sin of Adam was imputed upon us. But we should not get upset with Adam and Eve because we have done a lot of sinning ourselves. When God gets finished with forgiving me for what I've done, I will not even mention Adam. I'll just say, "Bless you, brother, and move on." But Adam's sin was laid upon me, and sin has a penalty. The penalty is eternal death. But yet I am saved. The saved are not saved from suffering. If you go to the hospitals you will find as many saved people there as you will those that are not saved. If you go to the nursing homes you will find as many feeble and weak saved people as those who are not saved. Sometime or another in this life we will all have to suffer. We are all dying physically, and that penalty we cannot escape. If we did not die physically then we would always live in a constant deteriorating state. When you're twenty-five years old, and your cheeks are rosy and your steps are swift, eternal life in your present body may seem all right. But when your eyes grow dim, and you began to suffer from afflictions, you won't mind moving from this house of clay. The saved are not saved from sorrow. There will come a time in your life where you will experience sadness. It may happen with the loss of a job or perhaps the loss of a loved one, but sorrow will come.

But not only are Christians saved from the penalty of sins, they are also being saved from the power of sin. It is related to your sanctification that is found in John 17:17 where John says, "Sanctify them by the truth; your word is truth." We are saved by the grace of God, and we are being saved every day of our lives. The Holy Spirit is constantly working on us. Positionally we are sanctified, but conditionally we are being sanctified. He's growing us every day, and He's making us smoother every day. He's shaping us into His very likeness. Every day of our lives we have the joy of getting better and better. Sin has power, and if you are not cognizant of it you will began to like it. Sin has control of the flesh and the inclinations of the flesh. If you are a human being in this world, there is a sin that you like. It is a besetting sin, and somehow it can get control of your innermost being. An alcoholic often says, "I wish I was not an alcoholic." Basically, he is saying that he has something that he cannot control. Paul testifies in Romans 7:14-17 that the things he hated he did, and the things that he didn't do and should have done he didn't do (paraphrased). It is because sin has control of the human flesh.

Lastly, we are saved from the wrath to come. Revelation 6:17 says, "For the great day of their wrath has come, and who is able to stand?" (NRSV). The world as we know it will not always be as it is now. This present world shall give way to a better world order. It will catch on fire and burn all imperfections. This present world order will be replaced with a divine world order. What we now see will not be there any longer. One great day God will step out in time and declare that the time that has been will not be that way anymore. When He does that, the Bible says the mountains shall skip like lambs into the waters. Water shall turn to blood. Boils shall break out from the top of people's heads to the bottom of their feet. We shall have tribulations like the world has never known. Many shall run and say, "Mountains, please fall on me." Many shall desire to die, but death will flee from them. But the saved are saved from the wrath of God because before the day of the wrath is the day of the Rapture. The saved will be caught up in the clouds to go and be with Christ and sit around His altar singing, "Holy, holy, holy." That is the gospel, and it is good news.

The Good News of Eschatology: Last Things

"What the caterpillar calls the end of the world, the master calls a butterfly."

Richard Bach (1936-)

The word "eschatology" comes from two Greek words, *eschatos*, meaning last, and *logos*, meaning Word. Therefore eschatology is the study of the last word or things that are to come. Paul says in 1 Thessalonians 4:13-18, "Brothers and sisters, we do not want you to be uninformed about those who sleep in death, so that you do not grieve like the rest of mankind, who have no hope. For we believe that Jesus died and rose again and so we believe that God will bring with Jesus those who have fallen asleep in him. According to the Lord's word, we tell you that we who are still alive, who are left until the coming of the Lord, will certainly not precede those who have fallen asleep. For the Lord himself will come down from heaven, with a loud command, with the voice of the archangel and with the trumpet call of God, and the dead in Christ will rise first. After that, we who are still alive and are left will be caught up together with them in the clouds to meet the Lord in the air. And so we will be with the Lord forever. Therefore encourage one another with these words" (NIV).

I cannot do justice to this topic without giving some historical implications. Christians in the first century AD believed the end of the world would come during their lifetime. In Mark 13:8, Jesus compared the end of the world with a mother's birth pain. The image implied that the world was already pregnant with its own destruction, but no one but God knows when it will happen. When the converts of Paul in Thessalonica were persecuted by the Roman Empire, they believed the end was upon them. However, doubt rose when as early as the 90s (AD) Christians said, "We have heard these things [of the end of the world] even in the days of our fathers, and look, we have grown old and none of them has happened to us." In the 130s (AD) Justin Martyr declared God was delaying the end of the world because he wished for Christianity to become a world religion. In the 250s (AD) Cyprian wrote that Christian sins of that time were a prelude and proof that the end was near.

However, by the third century most Christians believed the end was beyond their own lifetime; Jesus, it was believed, had denounced attempts to divine the future, to know the "times and seasons," and such attempts to predict the future were discouraged. Yet, the end was given a date with the help of Jewish traditions in the Six Ages of the World.

The Six Ages of the World is a Christian historical periodization first written by Saint Augustine circa 400 AD. It is based upon Christian religious events from the creation of Adam to the events of Revelation. The six ages of history, with each age lasting approximately one thousand years, were widely believed and in use throughout the Middle Ages, and until the Enlightenment, the writing of history was mostly the filling out of all or some part of the following outline. The Seventh Age (yet to come) being eternal rest after the final judgment and end-times, just as the seventh day of the week is reserved for rest. It was normally called the Six Ages of the World because they were the ages of the world, of history, while the Seventh Age was not of this world and would last forever. Saint Augustine describes these ages as follows.

The First Age: "The first is from the beginning of the human race, that is, from Adam, who was the first man that was made, down to Noah, who constructed the ark at the time of the flood."

The Second Age: "Extends from that period on to Abraham, who was called the father indeed of all nations " . . ."

The Third Age: "For the third age extends from Abraham on to David the king."

The Fourth Age: "The fourth from David on to that captivity whereby the people of God passed over into Babylonia."

The Fifth Age: "The fifth from that transmigration down to the advent of our Lord Jesus Christ."

The Sixth Age: "With His coming the sixth age has entered on its process."

Using this system, the end was fixed at 202, but when the date passed, the date was changed to 500 AD. After 500 AD the importance of the end as a part of Christianity was marginalized, though it continues to be stressed during the season of Advent. Currently, there are Christians who place the end of the world within their lifetime or shortly thereafter. Their convictions can sometimes be placed on the evidence of tragedies all around the world each day on the news, combined with interpretations of scriptures in the Bible.

Approximately 25 percent of the Bible is prophecy. Almost all of the things that the Bible prophesized to happen before Christ returns have already happened. No one knows the day or the hour as to when Christ will return. He has not shared that news with us. But he has told us something. In the last days, Christ is coming back to take His people home to heaven. This period is known as the Rapture. Christ will descend from heaven.

Revelation 1:1 says, "The revelation from Jesus Christ, which God gave him to show his servants what must soon take place. He made it known by sending his angel to his servant John." The word revelation derives from the Greek word *apokalupsis*. It means "an unveiling, revelation." It is the same Greek word from which we get the English word apocalyptic. If revelation means to unveil, then there must be something that was hidden. It is much like going into a room where the curtains are closed. When they are closed you cannot see very well, but when they are opened everything in that room is revealed, "an unveiling, revelation."

All Christian doctrines—the doctrine of sin, harmatology; the doctrine of the Holy Spirit, pneumatology; the doctrine of salvation, soteriology; the doctrine of God, theology; the doctrine of Christ, christology; the doctrine of the church, ecclesiology; and the doctrine of the end-times, eschatology—hinge on the fact that there is a hell to avoid and a heaven to gain.

So what does all of this mean to us? How should this affect the way we live our lives?

Eternal issues are at stake every time a person accepts or rejects Jesus Christ. The decision to accept or reject Jesus Christ is the biggest decision a person can ever make. Every other decision pales before it because every other decision has implications that end with death. But the realities of heaven and hell do not begin until the moment of death. A man may decide to marry a certain woman, and that decision will shape life for fifty years. He may decide to live in New York and not Miami, and that decision radically affects the course of his life. He may choose to go into kinesiology instead of taking over the family business, and that choice will follow him all the days of his life. But those choices—as momentous and life-shaping as they are—share this in common: their significance ends with the day of their death.

Ephesians 1:9 states, "He made known to us the mystery of his will according to his good pleasure, which he purposed in Christ." What is being said is that the truth of His revelation is unknowable, not because it is incomprehensible or mysterious but because it cannot be understood through intellectual speculation. The mystery of his purpose comes from divine revelation. The book of Revelation is God's final plan for His people. It tells us where we are going. So what's so good about eschatology? It makes us look to the Lord and his word with excitement and anticipation. It causes us to assess our lives now in the light of the future. We will all stand before the Judge at the bar of history.

Billy Graham said it best with these penetrating words, "God made man different from the other creatures. He made him in His own image, a living soul." When this body dies, and our earthly existence is terminated, the soul lives on forever. One thousand years from this day you will be more alive than you are at this moment. The Bible teaches that life does not end at the cemetery. There is a future life with God for those who put their trust in His Son, Jesus Christ. There is also a future hell of separation from God toward which all are going who have refused or neglected to receive His Son, Jesus Christ. God has more grace in his heart than you have sin in your life. Jesus is a better Savior than you are a sinner. You don't have to be a prisoner of your past. Somebody once said it this way. There will be three surprises when we get to heaven. Number one, we're going to be surprised that some people are there that we didn't expect to see there. Number two, we're going to be surprised that some people aren't there that we were sure were going to be there. Number three, the greatest surprise of all will be that we ourselves are there.

Conclusion

Everyone who has studied literature is familiar with the short story, the novel, the play, the poem, and the biography, as well as with other literary forms. But when Jesus Christ came to earth, a whole new category of literature was needed, and that category was the Gospels. The Gospels are not biographies, though they have strong biographical material. They are not stories, even though they contain stories such as the lost sheep and the prodigal son that are as interesting as any story you will find in all literature. The Gospels are not documentary reports, yet they contain accurate accounts of many conversations and discourses of our Lord.

But what you will find within the four Gospels—Matthew, Mark, Luke, and John—is a message of good news. When we speak of the Gospel of Luke, we ought to understand that it means the good news of Jesus Christ as recorded by Luke. There is but one Gospel, with four presentations. It is a message that says God saves sinners. Man is by nature sinful and separated from God with no hope of remedying that situation. But God, by His power, provided the means of man's redemption in the death, burial, and resurrection of the Savior, Jesus Christ. It's not that you must live differently or that you must follow a certain list of rules but that God will live inside you and change you into a new being. It's not that you have to go to a certain church, wear certain clothes, or pray in a certain way but that the Holy Spirit will live inside you and enable you to worship God in spirit and truth.

God has a free gift waiting for all humankind. You don't have to do anything to claim your gift of eternal life except to believe in your heart that Jesus died for your sins. It's like having a new Porsche waiting for you to pick up, but with this gift you don't have to leave home to claim it. You don't have to keep on living like you have no place at God's table; he's already reconciled your faults, and you can come on home. Now that's hope. That is grace. But most of all, that's good news.

There is a distressing tendency among many Christians to view the Gospel as useful only for conversion. In other words, the Gospel is viewed as a message that tells me how to be saved, but it is of little value in the area of Christian living. The fact is we need the Gospel just as much for Christian living as we do for salvation. Why? First because, as mentioned above, the Gospel easily slips through our fingers, and without our knowing it, we begin to depend on our efforts. Second, the Gospel is God's conduit of grace. The Gospel is not just information telling us how to be saved—it is "the power of God for salvation for everyone who believes" (Rom. 1:16; see also 1 Thess. 1:5, 1 Thess. 2. Through the Gospel, the Holy Spirit takes what Christ did two thousand years ago and brings it into the present. Through the Gospel, the Spirit works to create and sustain and grow our faith. According to scripture, God calls people to salvation through the Gospel (2 Thess. 2:14). According to scripture, the Gospel itself bears fruit and causes growth (Col. 1:6, Acts 20:32, and 1 Pet. 1:23).

Appendix

The Magnificence of God

O
bviously there were no buildings in the Garden of Eden—there is something magnificent about the creation of God in its pristine form. I'm always drawn to that. Yet, God allowed man to build places of worship, and I'm drawn to that as well. The following pages are a few of the places around the world where my wife Taryn and I saw and felt the magnificence of God.

Chapel of the Holy Cross, Sedona, Arizona
Photo courtesy of Taryn Bilberry

Chapel of Alto Vista, on the north coast of Aruba
Photo courtesy of Taryn Bilberry

St. Paul's Cathedral, London, England
Photo courtesy of Taryn Bilberry

St. Mary's Catholic Church, Virginia City, Nevada
Photo courtesy of Taryn Bilberry

Coliseum in Rome, Italy
Photo courtesy of Taryn Bilberry

Air Force Academy cadet chapel,
Colorado Springs, Colorado.
Photo courtesy of Taryn Bilberry

Blumenau, Brazil, Lutheran Church
Photo courtesy of Taryn Bilberry

Cathedral De Sao Sabastiao Do, Rio De Janeiro, Brazil
Photo courtesy of Charles Lee Bilberry

St. Peter's Basilica, Rome, Italy
Photo courtesy of Taryn Bilberry

Glacier near Seward, Alaska
Photo courtesy of Taryn Bilberry

Bryce Canyon, Utah
Photo courtesy of Taryn Bilberry

Westminster Abbey, London, England
Photo courtesy of Taryn Bilberry

Corcovada (Christ the Redeemer)
Rio De Janeiro, Brazil
Photo courtesy of Taryn Bilberry

Corcovada (Christ the Redeemer)
Rio De Janeiro, Brazil
Photo courtesy of Taryn Bilberry

Napoli coastline, Kauai, Hawaii
Photo courtesy of Taryn Bilberry

Mexico Mission T (building a home)
Tijuana, Mexico
Photo courtesy of Taryn Bilberry

Pyramid of Kukulcan at Chichen Itza,
near Cancun, Mexico
Photo courtesy of Taryn Bilberry

East coast of South America, ocean sunrise
Photo courtesy of Taryn Bilberry

Cruise ship docked in Roseau, Dominica
Photo courtesy of Taryn Bilberry

Grand Canyon National Park south rim,
Grand Canyon, Arizona
Photo courtesy of Taryn Bilberry

Tivoli Gardens, Copenhagen, Denmark
Photo courtesy of Taryn Bilberry

Sedona, Arizona, landscape
Photo courtesy of Taryn Bilberry

Stalagmites and stalactites at Lehman Caves,
Great Basin National Park, near Ely, Nevada
Photo courtesy of Taryn Bilberry

Washington Monument, Washington, DC
Photo courtesy of Taryn Bilberry

Costa Rican beach near Manuel Antonio National Park
Photo courtesy of Taryn Bilberry

Fish and coral near Puerto Morelos, Mexico
Photo courtesy of Charles Lee Bilberry

Yosemite National Park, California
Photo courtesy of Taryn Bilberry

Works Cited

Unless otherwise indicated, all references are taken from the New International Version of the Bible. The use of footnotes has been avoided in order to conserve space. Instead, parenthetical references for quoted material and references to other works that are suggested for further study have been given. These references will include the following works:

Aldrich, Joe. 1999. *Lifestyle Evangelism*. Colorado Springs, CO: Multnomah Books.

Bauer, Walter. 1979. *A Greek-English Lexicon of the New Testament and Other Early Christian Literature*. Chicago: The University of Chicago Press.

Gilbert, Gregory D. 2010. *What is the Gospel?* Wheaton, IL: Crossway Books.

Grudem, Wayne. 2011. *Making Sense of Salvation: One of Seven Parts from Grudem's Systematic Theology (Making Sense of Series)*. Grand Rapids, MI: Zondervan.

Hobbs, Herschel H. 1960. *Fundamentals of Our Faith*. Nashville, TN: Broadman and Holman Publishers.

Mears, Henrietta C. 1966. *What the Bible Is All About*. Glendale, CA: Regal Books.

Moody Bible Study Helps. 1951. *What Christians Believe*. Chicago: Moody Press.

Sproul, R. C. 2010. *Saved From What?* Wheaton, IL: Crossway Publishers.

Stanton, Graham N. 1989. *The Gospels and Jesus*. New York: Oxford University Press.

Woodroof, Tim. Archive for the *"What is the Gospel?" Essays*. Tim Woodroof.com.